The Gloucester Book...

Frank L. Cox

Nabu Public Domain Reprints:

You are holding a reproduction of an original work published before 1923 that is in the public domain in the United States of America, and possibly other countries. You may freely copy and distribute this work as no entity (individual or corporate) has a copyright on the body of the work. This book may contain prior copyright references, and library stamps (as most of these works were scanned from library copies). These have been scanned and retained as part of the historical artifact.

This book may have occasional imperfections such as missing or blurred pages, poor pictures, errant marks, etc. that were either part of the original artifact, or were introduced by the scanning process. We believe this work is culturally important, and despite the imperfections, have elected to bring it back into print as part of our continuing commitment to the preservation of printed works worldwide. We appreciate your understanding of the imperfections in the preservation process, and hope you enjoy this valuable book.

A MODERN BANK AT YOUR SERVICE

An ideal location, an unsurpassed equipment and an efficient organization combined with a desire to be of genuine service to this community is what we offer.

Our modern massive vaults will appeal to you.

SAFE DEPOSIT BOXES TO RENT AT $3.00 A YEAR

GLOUCESTER NATIONAL BANK
OLDEST BANK IN THE COUNTY
—Est. 1796—

F. J. BABSON & CO.,
INSURANCE

GLOUCESTER SAFE DEPOSIT & TRUST CO. BUILDING

DELIVERIES MADE TO

Essex

Magnolia

Manchester

West Gloucester

and all parts of the Cape

Telephone 66——666

HART GARAGE COMPANY,
COMPLETE
Electrical and Mechanical
SERVICE

Telephone 1609

15 EAST MAIN STREET

GLOUCESTER, - MASS.

Official { BOSCH / REMY / GRAY & DAVIS / ATWATER-KENT / DELCO } Service and Sales

THE BIG OUTSTANDING BANK
OF GLOUCESTER

Has a Department for Each Branch of Banking

Combined Assets of All Departments

FIVE AND ONE-HALF MILLIONS

Service With Safety

Gloucester Safe Deposit & Trust Co.

At Sunset

Copyright,
Frank L.

Artistic Photographs
of Gloucester

in Black and White, Sepia and Colors

by Frank L. Cox

*

For Sale at
   Nunes' Art Store, 8 Centre St.
   Grace Horne's Studio, E. Gloucester

*

A selection of six typical Gloucester scenes on finest imported photo paper, size 6 1-2 by 8 1-2, sent on receipt of $5.00. Frank L. Cox, Fernwood, Gloucester.

PARKHURST FISHERIES CO.

GLOUCESTER, - MASS.

Wholesale Dealers in all kinds of

Salt, Dried, Smoked, Canned and Pickled Fish.

Taking Fish at Traps at our Branch in Ingonish, C. B.

PARKHURST SALT CO.

Wholesale Dealers in

Domestic and Foreign Salts.

DISTRIBUTING BRANCH:

Pierce, Austin-Caswell, Livermore Co.

BOSTON, - MASS.

COPYRIGHT, 1921
By Frank L. Cox,
Fernwood, Gloucester, Mass.

Harbor Cove, Gloucester

Copyright, 1921
Frank L. Cox

The GLOUCESTER BOOK

Written and Illustrated
by Frank L. Cox

White & Gaffney, Inc.
Printers
Gloucester, Mass.

The writer of this little book wishes to express his appreciation to all those who have helped by their interest and kindly criticism in its preparation. He extends his thanks to the advertisers for their hearty co-operation and asks for them a generous share of the reader's patronage.

History of Gloucester.

Famed in song and story, Gloucester, the pioneer fishing town of America, has been endowed with a wealth of natural beauty which added to the quaint charm of its picturesque waterfront and the sturdy personalities of its seafaring men make it a land of romance to the visitor.

The first visit of the white man to the shores of Cape Ann of which we have any authentic record was made by Champlain, in July, 1605, when he made a landing where Rockport now stands. The early records of that visit tell us that he was kindly received by the Indians, who told him by signs something of the geography of the country roundabout. He returned to Cape Ann in 1606, in September, and sailed into Gloucester harbor, which he named Le Beauport, the beautiful harbor. On the occasion of this second visit he did not find the Indians so hospitable and remained only long enough to make some necessary repairs to his ship. A party of sailors who had made a landing were attacked by the Indians but returned to their vessel unharmed after driving the Indians off

In 1623, the first settlement on Cape Ann was established by fourteen fishermen and farmers, sent out by the Dorchester Company, of Dorchester, England. They landed at Half Moon Beach, a part of what is today called Stage Fort park. In the early days this tract of land was called Fishermen's Field, from the fact that the first fishing stage was erected here. In 1907, a bronze tablet was placed here on a huge boulder near the landing place, by the citizens of Gloucester, with the following inscription —

ON THIS SITE IN
1623
A Company of Fishermen and Farmers from Dorchester,
England, under the direction of Rev. John White
founded
THE MASSACHUSETTS BAY COLONY
From that time, the Fisheries, the oldest industry in
the Commonwealth have been uninterruptedly
pursued from this Port.
Here in 1625 Governor Roger Conant by wise diplomacy
averted bloodshed between contending factions,
one led by Miles Standish of Plymouth,
the other by Capt. Hewes.
A Notable Exemplification of Arbitration in the
Beginnings of the New World.

This first attempt to establish a colony on Cape Ann was a failure, and a majority of those who came in 1623 returned to England in 1625, others with Roger Conant, joining the colony at Salem.

The few courageous settlers who remained were joined by others from time to time until in 1642 the settlement was incorporated as a town and named Gloucester, after Gloucester, England, from whence a large number of the latest settlers had come.

The early settlers of Gloucester were not molested by the Indians, and in this respect they were more fourtnate than the colonies at Plymouth and Boston. The large numbers of them mentioned by Champlain on his visits in 1605 and 1606 to the shores of Cape Ann, had evidently moved to another part of New England or had been wiped out by a pestilence for there is no mention of them in the early records of the colony.

That they once had a village on Cape Ann there is little doubt as many evidences of their former existence here in the shape of stone arrow heads, pipes, and stone hatchets have been dug up by gardeners and builders at Wheeler's Point and in the vicinity of Wingaersheek Beach. What is thought to have been an old Indian burying ground was discovered at Annisquam some years ago when some workmen unearthed ten skulls believed to have been those of Indians.

It is interesting to dream back to those days of long ago and to know that where some of the most flourishing summer colonies on Cape Ann are today, the Indians once built their wigwams and planted their corn.

General View of Gloucester

Before Gloucester had become a town a meeting house had been erected (1633) on what is now Beacon Hill The first minister of whom there is any record was the Rev. Richard Blynman, who joined the colony in 1642, coming from Plymouth. The reverend gentleman must have been somewhat of an engineer also for he planned and made the excavations from the Squam river to the harbor, now called the "Cut," thus making Gloucester an island. The present bridge over the "Cut" on Western avenue is named after him. Although he is spoken of in the early records as a man of sweet disposition and humble ways, his stay in the colony was a stormy one as the church meetings were frequently broken up and his ministry was marked by other disturbances. He left the ministry here and moved to New London in 1650.

The fisheries were well established between 1630 and 1640 and have been carried on steadily in Gloucester up to the present time. A detailed account of the fishing industry is given in a separate chapter.

Along with the fishing industry came ship building and as early as 1643 we read of a ship being built here for a Mr. Griffin. In the early days Cape Ann was heavily wooded with an abundance of oak, which furnished excellent material for the construction of ships.

There is an interesting story connected with the first vessel of the "schooner" type. Andrew Robinson, descendant of Abraham Robinson who settled in Gloucester in 1631, and a leading ship builder of the town, pursued his trade at a shipyard located near the old ferry landing in East Gloucester. In 1713 he had completed a vessel designed by himself and built and rigged along entirely new lines. As the boat slid down the stocks and struck the water a bystander remarked, "See how she scoons." "A schooner let her be" rejoined Robinson, as he broke a bottle of rum over her bow, and thus a new name was added to the mercantile vocabulary and a new rig to the commerce of the world.

As early as 1635, a shipwreck, terrible and pathetic in its details, occured just off the coast at Thacher's Island. On the 14th of August, 1635, a pinnace bound from Ipswich to Marblehead, and having on board the Rev. John Avery and Mr. Anthony Thacher, with their families, and a crew of four, was wrecked on the rocks of Thacher's Island. Twenty lives were lost, the only persons saved being Thacher and his wife. After spending two days on the island they managed to attract the attention of a passing vessel and were taken to Marblehead. The island was originally named Thacher's Woe. The twin lighthouses

were erected in 1771 and were lighted for the first time on December 21st of that year.

Witchcraft did not reach as serious a stage in Gloucester as it did in Boston and Salem, altho in 1692 six women of the town were accused of being witches and imprisoned. One of the first to be accused was Abigail Somes, who was confined in Boston for seven months and finally released without trial.

By 1700, much progress had been made in the development of the town. The population at that time was about 650 people. Churches and schools had been established, saw mills and grist mills had been built and many of the early log cabins had been replaced by the more substantial and comfortable frame houses. The chief industries of the town were the fisheries, ship building, and farming.

For the first hundred years the town selectmen did not receive any fixed salary for their services but were paid according to the time they gave to the business of the town. They did not meet frequently, but when they had business to transact it was customary to meet at one of the town taverns, and as these meetings generally lasted for a whole day at a time a bill for meals and drink was rendered to the town at the end of the year. On one occasion, when the town officials were sworn in in 1740, the "expenses for the selectmen and 'licker' at the house of Mr. James Stevens were L3. 18s. 2d." The Stevens tavern was the first tavern in Gloucester. It is still standing on Washington street and is known today as the old Ellery House.

In March, 1744, war was declared between England and France. Louisburg, on the island of Cape Breton, was held by the French who had spent many years and considerable money to fortify it, making it practically impregnable. As long as the French remained in possesion it was a menace to the fishing vessels of Gloucester and the other colonies of New England. It was determined to attack this French stronghold and accordingly a force of about 4000 men, most of them from Massachusetts, under command of William Pepperell, joined forces with the British and effected the surrender of the city and fortress on June 16th, 1745.

Gloucester's part in the expedition against Louisburg would not be complete without the story of Peg Wesson. She was reputed to be a witch and lived in the old Garrison House on Prospect street where the Parochial residence now stands. Some soldiers from Captain Blyle's company, feeling in a jovial mood paid a visit to the famous

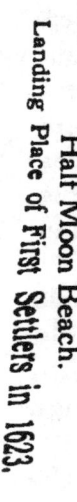

Half Moon Beach.
Landing Place of First Settlers in 1623.
Copyright, Frank L. Cox

witch just previous to their departure for Cape Breton. Soldier fashion they joked with and bantered her, until finally losing her temper she uttered a terrific oath, told them they would repent of their folly and threatened them with vengeance at Louisburg. Laughing scornfully, they departed and thought no more of the incident until some months later. One day when they were in camp at Louisburg they saw a crow flying just over their heads and were attracted by its peculiar actions. After a number of shots had been fired in a vain attempt to kill the bird, one of the soldiers, remembering the threat of Peg Wesson to visit them suggested that it must be her in one of her disguises. It was a well known fact that only a bullet of silver or gold would put an end to a witch and for a moment the soldiers were perplexed. But for a moment only as one of them soon produced a silver cuff button, rammed it into his gun, took careful aim and fired. The bird fell, with a broken leg. It was not until their return to Gloucester that the men found that their suspicions of Peg Wesson's connection with the crow were verified for at the very moment that the crow had been shot down the witch had fallen and broken her leg and they learned that in dressing the wound the surgeon had been astounded to discover in the wound a silver cuff button.

By 1750 the population of Gloucester had increased to 2700 people and the town was in a thriving condition. The fisheries were firmly established and a substantial source of revenue in connection with the commerce which was being carried on with the colonies and foreign countries.

What had originally been a mere path in the woods was now the principal business thoroughfare, Fore street (the Main street of today), the land along the harbor front had been cleared of trees and a number of wharves built. The fishing fleet together with the vessels engaged in foreign trade numbered about seventy-five good sized vessels at this time.

The Revolutionary period and shortly after was a time of privation and hardship for Gloucester as well as the rest of the colonies. Many of the fishing vessels were fitted out as privateers and a large number were either captured or destroyed by the British, with a consequent heavy loss of life among the crews. On the other hand several hundred British ships were taken by the combined fleet of American privateers. The fisheries and commerce were temporarily destroyed and the town became heavily in debt. Prices of general merchandise were exhorbitant

Schooner Natalie Hammond.

Copyright, 1921
Frank L. Cox

and profiteering was carried on freely. A paper dollar at that time was worth about three cents. Within a short time after peace returned the fisheries were again being carried on vigorously and foreign commerce had been restored with Europe and the West Indies, reaching its highest point between 1790 and 1810. The population in 1800 was about 5300.

In 1774 a notable event in the history of religion occurred in Gloucester when the Rev. John Murray was invited to the town and began preaching the doctrines of Universalism. His preaching met with considerable opposition and finally in 1776 he was requested to leave town, after a mob had gathered in front of the Sargent house on Main street where the meetings were held and threatened him with violence if he remained. He paid little attention to their demands and after a short time continued his preaching to the little group who had remained faithful to him.

In 1778 the First Church suspended fifteen of its members who had joined the Universalists. In answer to this Universalists drew up a series of Articles setting forth their rights as follows: as an "Independent Christian Church of Christ, resolved by God's grace to meet together, whether blessed with the public preaching of the word or not, to meet together to supplicate the Divine favor, to praise our redeeming God, to hear His most holy word and freely to communicate whatever God shall please to manifest to us for our mutual edification."

In 1780 they erected the first Universalist meeting house at the corner of Main and Water streets. The present church on Middle street was erected in 1805-6.

From the period just after the Civil War to 1874 there was a marked increase in the population and prosperity of the town. In the latter year Gloucester was incorporated as a city and elected Robert R. Fears first mayor. In all the troublous days of the nation from the Revolutionary period down through the years to the recent World War, Gloucester has been well represented in the army and navy, and has proudly and gladly borne her share in helping to make glorious the history of our country.

By reason of its rocky nature Cape Ann has never been an agricultural region, and so in the future as in the past, must look to the fisheries as the principal means of its sustenance. There are, however, other interests which have been developed and are important elements in the growth of the city. Gloucester stands today as one of the most prosperous and progessive cities in the Commonwealth, and backed with the traditions of a glorious past looks forward with confidence into the future.

Dogtown and Its Story.

Over a century has passed since the sounds of habitation were last heard in the deserted village of Dogtown and but little now remains save the old roads which ran through the center of the village, and here and there traces of old cellars that mark the sites of the little homes where the inhabitants of this quaint community once lived.

There is much of mystery and romance, and a certain charm about this old abandoned hamlet which one cannot help but feel in walking about through the wilderness of boulders that surrounds Dogtown on every side. Very little is known of the early history of the settlement and there have been many conjectures as to the reasons why the settlers should have decided to build their homes on such a remote and barren plain.

While the land cost little or nothing and was considered practically worthless it could be used for pasturage and would yield vegetables, and as many of the early families were in poor circumstances it afforded them a chance to establish a home at very small cost. Most of the homes were occupied during the Revolutionary War by the families of men who were serving as soldiers or sailors in those stirring days, and for years after, the widows of many of these brave men continued to live in their gambrel-roofed houses and formed the large majority of the inhabitants.

The best approach to Dogtown, coming from Gloucester, is by way of Gee avenue at Riverdale. After passing a number of typical Cape

Note: — The stranger has the choice of several routes to visit Dogtown, namely: take conveyance from Gloucester and follow along Washington street to Poplar street, Reynard street, or Gee avenue. The Gee avenue route is recommended as the shortest and most interesting.

A Wilderness of Boulders.

Ann farmhouses the avenue gradually narrows down to a rocky lane with great grey boulders on either side, and in a short time the heart of Dogtown is reached.

One has to look sharp to find any signs of what was at one time a

Foundation Stones of a Dogtown House.

thriving little settlement, for the only inhabitants of Dogtown today are a few cattle which graze among its rocks and small trees, as the cattle of the inhabitants did many years ago. It is not hard, however, if one is patient and persistent enough, to find traces of what were once houses, for the foundation stones of about fifty dwellings are to be seen, most of the old cellars being filled in with earth and covered with a growth of small trees and grass.

There are no authentic figures available which give the population of Dogtown but the best estimates place it at about one hundred families. As this number formed a fair sized village in those days it seems probable that there must have been a schoolhouse and at least one church there also but no traces or records of these are to be found.

The people who built and lived in Dogtown were those who had in their veins the best blood of Gloucester, and many of the old families, prominent in the life of the city today, trace their ancestry back to the deserted village.

Just to the left of the road at the top of a small hill as one enters from Gee avenue is one of the most celebrated cellar in Dogtown. It is that of John Morgan Stanwood, who was mistakenly made famous by a poem by Hiram Rich, published in the Atlantic some years ago.

> "Morgan Stanwood, patriot,
>   Little more is known:
> Nothing of his home is left
>   But the door-step stone.
>
> Morgan Stanwood, to our thought
>   You return once more;
> Once again the meadows lift
>   Daisies to your door.
>
> Once again the morn is sweet,
>   Half the hay is down:—
> Hark! What means that sudden clang
>   From the distant town?
>
> Larum bell and rolling drum
>   Answer sea-borne guns;
> Larum bell and rolling drum
>   Summon Freedom's sons.

* * * *

> Down the musket comes. 'Good wife—
>   Wife a quicker flint!'
> And the face that questions face
>   Hath no color in 't.
>
> * * * *
>
> Morgan Stanwood sped along,
>   Not the common road;
> Over wall and hill top straight,
>   Straight for death, he strode."

The poem refers to an event during the Revolutionary war. On August 8th, 1775, the British sloop-of-war Falcon chased an American vessel, bound from the West Indies to Salem, into Gloucester Harbor, where she grounded near Five Pound Island. Captain Lindsay of the Falcon anchored his sloop in the harbor and determined to take the American boat captive, but the troops on shore were equally determined that the boat would not be taken and put up such a stubborn resistance, killing and capturing a large number of the men he had sent to take the boat, that he was compelled to withdraw the next day. During the engagement one American, Benjamin Rowe, was killed, and another, Peter Lurvey, was mortally wounded.

As Morgan Stanwood was not born until about 1774, he could not have taken part in the fight, and the hero of the poem should have been Peter Lurvey. On the morning of that fatal day Lurvey with his wife and a neighbor's daughter were over on Pearce's Island picking huckleberries and when he heard the alarm he hurriedly bade his wife good-bye, rowed to the opposite shore, ran to the house and grabbed his gun and quickly joined the other patriots in Gloucester, where he met his death. Lurvey's house was quite a distance in from the Dogtown road on the left, on the top of a hill, from which there is a wonderful view of Annisquam and Ipswich Bay. Near the old cellar is the old well, now completely filled in, and the foundation stones of what was probably a barn. The land is well cleared of rocks and must have been an excellent place to raise vegetables and grain. This is the most interesting site in all Dogtown but difficult for a stranger to find as it is some distance in from the road and there is no well defined path leading to it. John Morgan Stanwood married Lurvey's daughter and this fact probably led to the confusion of the two in Rich's poem.

"Tammy" Younger, "Queen of the Witches," and one of the most noted characters of Dogtown, was born on July 28, 1753, and lived, until her death in 1829, in a house on Cherry street, on what was then the main thoroughfare from Gloucester to Annisquam and Lanesville. She had the reputation of using very strong language at times and was very much respected and feared in the village.

A Dogtown Road

If she heard a team going by her house it was her habit to boldly cry out to the driver and find out what he was carrying. If it was anything she took a fancy to, such as food or wood she would often demand some, and woe be to him who refused her. She had an aunt living in the same house, "Luce George," who, tradition tells us, used to stand at the door of her little house and when a team of oxen was going by, would bewitch them so that they would come to a stop and be unable to come up the hill until a portion of the grain or fish on the team had been unloaded at her door. It is said she would often visit the wharves in Gloucester and when a vessel came in laden with fish she would demand enough to last her for several days.

Just beyond where Tammy Younger lived was the old blacksmith shop, kept by Joseph Allen, who came to Gloucester in 1674. He was married twice and had seventeen children.

"Easter" Carter, another noted character, lived in a two story house near the center of the village. She was very poor but quite respectable and resented any allusion to her poverty. It was a common custom in those days for the young people to take their lunches with them and spend the day at her little farm, getting her to boil cabbage for them, and partake of their dinner under the trees in picnic style. Dinner over she would sit and tell their fortunes and the day would be finished by a stroll home through the weird rock strewn pastures in the moonlight.

A Dogtown Cellar

These are but a few of the characters and traditions that memory has handed down to us through the years. Space forbids a detailed account of the many other interesting inhabitants and their homes here.

When the bridge was built at Riverdale, it diverted travel from what had been the main road through Dogtown to Annisquam and Lanesville, to Washington street. From that time the little village gradually began to decline and in time was deserted altogether. What Goldsmith has said in his beautifully pathetic "Deserted Village" may well be said of Dogtown —

"Sweet was the sound, when oft at evening's close
Up yonder hill the village murmur rose.
There, as I passed with careless steps and slow,
The mingling notes came softened from below;

The swain responsive as the milkmaid sung,
The sober herd that lowed to meet their young,
The noisy geese that gabbled o'er the pool,
The playful children just let loose from school."

    *   *   *   *   *

"But now the sounds of population fail,
No cheerful murmurs fluctuate in the gale,
No busy steps the grass-grown foot-way tread,
But all the bloomy flush of life is fled."

30 THE GLOUCESTER BOOK

Two of the Main Streets and General View of Gloucester, England

Photos by Chris Johns and Sidney A. Pitcher
Gloucester, England

Interesting Facts Concerning Gloucester, England

Gloucester, England, for which city Gloucester, Massachusetts, is named, is a city of over 50,000 people, situated on the east bank of the river Severn, about 114 miles north-west of London. It is the most inland port in England and has splendid waterway communications with the chief manufacturing centres of the Midlands.

It carries on an extensive trade with many countries, imports consisting of timber, grain, seed oil-cake, bones, guano, clay, marble, sugar, and general cargo from Canada, Argentine, and the Continent. The exports consists of coal, salt, pitch, iron, slate, bricks, and earthenware, being sent to the Continent, East Indies, Australia, and other parts of the world.

The ancient city, apart from its chief treasure, the Cathedral, is, historically, one of the most interesting places in England. There is evidence that Gloucester was an inhabited place long before the Romans came to Britain and that probably the Latin invaders themselves, when they came there, found a community established upon the site.

It was about fifty years after the birth of Christ that the Roman conquest of Britain actively began, and eventually the Romans in their increasing grip upon the country came to the banks of the Severn, and, no doubt, recognizing the military value of the site of the city, they built upon it a strong walled camp the better to overawe and keep in subjection the Britons whom they had driven before them to the west.

Then came the fall of Rome and for an interval of hundreds of years history does not record what happened, until we read of it again in the time of the Saxons. Since the old troublous days the story of Gloucester has been mainly a record of commercial and civic expansion, the fortunes of the city have grown apace, and each succeeding reign has witnesses great developments.

Gloucester Cathedral ranks high among the cathedral churches of England and is a splendid example of the art and skill possessed by the builders of early days. The Cathedral site has been occupied by a sacred edifice since the year 681, and part of the present structure dates from about 1089.

From the "Official Handbook of Gloucester, England."

Tall Pines—Ravenswood
Norman's Woe
U. S. Coast Guard Station

Points of Interest.

Interesting Walks and Rides, Historic Old Houses, Places of Scenic and Historic Interest.

AROUND THE CAPE

For a trip of great scenic interest the following route is recommended—Start from Washington street corner of Main by automobile and continue along Washington through Riverdale, Annisquam, Bay View, Lanesville, Pigeon Cove, Rockport, and return to Gloucester.

BLYNMAN BRIDGE

Marks the site on Western avenue where the excavations were made by the Rev. Richard Blynman, first minister of the town, in 1643. The "Cut," through which flows the waters of the Squam river to the outer harbor, makes Gloucester an island.

COMMERCIAL STREET

A walk down Commercial street and out on to some of the old wharves which lead from it on the left hand side gives one an interesting glimpse of the Italian fishermen, and their picturesque boats. It is a favorite section of the artists during the summer season.

DOG BAR BREAKWATER

At the extreme end of Eastern point. It gives Gloucester one of the safest harbors in this country. During it's erection there were several wrecks on its rocks. It is nearly half a mile long, built of Cape Ann granite, and was finished in 1904.

FERNWOOD LAKE

A pretty little lake about eight minutes walk from the West Gloucester railroad station. A good starting point for a walk through the woods to Ravenswood park and Western avenue.

FIRST TOWN HALL

The first town hall was built in 1844, and for many years had been in use as a school. In 1920 it was presented by the city to Capt Lester S. Wass Post, No. 3, of the American Legion. It is located on Washington street, corner Middle street.

FIVE AND TEN POUND ISLANDS

These islands were originally bought from the Indians for the respective sums, five and ten pounds, from which they derived their names. In 1887 the United States Fish Commission established a station on Ten Pound Island which is used as a fish hatchery and for experiments in the propagation of various kinds of salt water fish. A lighthouse was erected on the same island in 1820.

FORT SQUARE

The site of the first fort, built in Gloucester in 1742, and occupied during the Revolutionary War and the War of 1812. Located at the end of Commercial street.

GOOD HARBOR BEACH

One of the finest beaches in Gloucester, situated between Bass Rocks and Brier Neck. In January 1796, it was the scene of a distressing shipwreck when a Boston ship, the "Industry," went ashore near Salt Island during a violent snow-storm and all hands were lost.

GOVERNOR'S HILL

At the top of Commonwealth avenue, was in the Revolutionary days called Beacon Pole hill because it was used at that time to give warning, by means of beacon lights, of the approach of enemy ships. An exceptionally fine view of Gloucester harbor may be had from the little park at the top.

MOUNT ANNE

The highest point of land on Cape Ann, is located in West Gloucester and affords a wonderful view from the top, of Gloucester and the country round about for many miles.

NORMAN'S WOE

Between Magnolia and Fresh Water Cove, just off the coast, where several wrecks have taken place in the past, and made famous by Longfellow's poem, "The Wreck of the Hesperus." In connection with the poem the following extract taken from Longfellow's diary is interesting—

"December 17, 1839 — News of shipwrecks horrible on the coast. Twenty bodies washed ashore near Gloucester, one lashed to a piece of the wreck. There is a reef called Norman's Woe, where many of them took place, among others the schooner Hesperus, also the Sea Flower on Black Rock. I must write a ballad upon this, also upon two others, "The Skeleton in Armor" and "Sir Humphrey Davy"

OLD BURYING GROUND

Located on Centennial avenue, in which many of the early settlers were buried. It was used as early as 1642 and is the oldest in the city.

Old Fort—Stage Fort Park.

OLD MOTHER ANN

A remarkable formation in the boulders on the shore at Eastern Point near the lighthouse resembling the face and figure of an old woman.

RAFE'S CHASM

A remarkable fissure in the rock on the shore a short distance from Magnolia. It is over two hundred feet long and sixty feet deep.

RAVENSWOOD PARK

A beautiful woodland tract of several hundred acres, with fine roads, well laid out by-paths and pretty rustic bridges. Situated to the left of Western avenue, entering the city   The old Salem Turnpike, over which Governor Roger Conant and his followers went to join the colony at Salem in 1625, runs through the park and passes "The Hermitage," where the noted hermit naturalist, Mason Walton lived for thirty years.

RIVERDALE

Just over the bridge at the left on Washington street are the old mills, one of which was erected about 1677 and has been in use as a corn mill since that time   The first saw mill was erected on this site in 1642.

SALT ISLAND

A short distance off shore from Good Harbor beach and easily reached from there by walking at low tide. It has been used in the past as a setting for a number of moving picture productions.

STAGE FORT PARK

The most historic tract of land on Cape Ann, is located at the right of Western avenue at the entrance to Gloucester. In 1623, the first settlement was established here, which is commemorated by a tablet erected by the citizens of Gloucester in 1907 on the large boulder near Half Moon beach. (Referred to in chapter on "History of Gloucester"). A fort was erected here in 1775 and was occupied during the Revolutionary War, the War of 1812, the Civil War, and the Spanish-American War in 1898.

SUNSET ROCK

A high boulder at Riverview a short walk from Washington street, affording a fine view of Annisquam, the river, and Ipswich Bay.

THACHERS ISLAND

A long narrow island, now owned by the government, off Lands End, Rockport. The twin lights were lighted for the first time on December 21, 1771. For detailed account see chapter on "History of Gloucester."

UNITARIAN (FIRST PARISH) CHURCH

The present church on Middle street was built in 1828 on the site of the church built there in 1738. The town meetings and all important public meetings were held in the older church during the latter part of the eighteenth and the early part of the nineteenth centuries. The present church contains many interesting historical relics, among them, the shot which was fired into the old church in August, 1775, by the

British Man of War, Falcon, and a rare silver communion service over a hundred years old.

UNITED STATES COAST GUARD STATION

At Fresh Water Cove, where a constant guard is maintained, day and night, for vessels and small boats in distress.

UNITED STATES NAVAL COMPASS STATION

Near the Coast Guard station at Fresh Water Cove, furnishes radio compass bearings to all classes of vessels equipped with wireless within a radius of 150 miles. This service is of great value to navigators during storms and foggy weather.

UNIVERSALIST CHURCH (Independent Christian Society)

The present church on Middle street was built in 1806 and is one of the most interesting buildings in Gloucester from a historical and religious standpoint. It was here that Rev. John Murray, founder of Universalism in America, preached, and after him Rev. Thomas Jones, and the church contains many articles of interst in connection with these first ministers. The church bell was cast in the foundry of Paul Revere. Among the most interesting relics are the old barrel organ which was used in the first meeting place of Murray and his followers, a beautiful colonial clock and a communion service over a hundred years old. See chapter on "History of Gloucester" for further account.

WHIPPING POST

Site of the old Whipping Post which was used for the last time in 1780, is at the corner of Hancock and Middle streets and is now occupied by the Y. M. C. A. building.

WINGAERSHEEK BEACH

A beach of fine white sand backed by dunes of huge size and remarkable beauty, between the Annisquam and Ipswich rivers. The beach is located in West Gloucester and can be reached from Essex avenue by turning in at Concord or Atlantic street, or by ferry from Annisquam. It was originally called Coffin's beach, it's owner, Peter Coffin, having settled in Gloucester in 1688.

For information concerning Annisquam, Bass Rocks, Eastern Point, Magnolia, and Rockport, see chapter on "Summer Colonies."

Old Colonial Houses and Taverns.

Gloucester is rich in beautiful old colonial houses, but to tell the story of all of them with their interesting histories and traditions would require a much larger volume than this one. A brief description and history of a few of the most noted is all that space will allow in this little book.

Sargent-Murray-Gilman House. The most noted as well as the most beautiful old colonial house on Cape Ann is located at 47 Middle street. The interior of the house, which has been changed but little from the time it was built, is remarkably well preserved and the beautiful stairway with its hand carved balusters and panelling has few, if any superiors in New England. The house was erected about 1768 but historians differ as to who the builder was. It is a fact, however, that the house was owned by Winthrop Sargent, the most prominent merchant in Gloucester at that time, for it was sold to Frederick Gilman in 1797 by his heirs, including John and Judith (Sargent) Murray. Judith Sargent was the daughter of Winthrop Sargent and first married John Stevens, and after his death she became the wife of John Murray, founder of Universalism in America. She was a beautiful, talented woman and a writer of ability. The house should be of interest to all Harvard men for it was here that the Rev. Samuel Gilman, author of "Fair Harvard," was born. For further facts concerning John Murray and Universalism see chapter on "History of Gloucester."

Riggs House. The oldest house on Cape Ann, located on Vine street, Annisquam, was built in 1660 by Thomas Riggs, the first schoolmaster and town clerk of Gloucester. The house is a good example of the dwellings erected by the early settlers, and was originally constructed of squared logs.

Sawyer Free Library. Located on Middle street, it was built in 1764 and presented to the city in 1884 by Samuel E. Sawyer to be used as a

OLD COLONIAL HOUSES AND TAVERNS 39

library. Previous to its use as a library it was known as the Sanders House. Its beautiful colonial interiors have been preserved.

Ellery House, Located at 244 Washington street, it was built in 1704 by Rev. John White, minister of the First Parish. Later it was sold to James Stevens, who kept it as a tavern until 1740, when it was bought by William Ellery. Before a Town Hall was built it was the custom of the Selectmen to hold their meetings at one of the town taverns, and the Stevens Tavern, as it was called at the time, was used for this purpose on many occasions and the "expense for the Selectmen and Licker at the house of Mr. James Stevens" was paid by the town.

Sargent-Murrry-Gilman House—Right

The house is still owned and occupied by the descendants of William Ellery.

Babson House. On the opposite side of the street from the Ellery House at number 245 Washington, built in 1749. An interesting feature of this house is the old slave pens in the attic, used when slavery existed here.

Epes Sargent House. Originally located at the corner of Main and Pleasant streets, where the Post Office now stands was the mansion of Colonel Epes Sargent. It was occupied by his descendants for two generations and then sold to Nathaniel Webster. It is now on Liberty street where it was moved about thirty years ago.

Broome Tavern. One of the most noted taverns on Cape Ann during the early part of the 18th century. It was kept by James Broome who came here from England in 1721. In connection with the tavern he kept a barber shop and his daughter, Rebecca, who became an expert barber carried on the business in a shop at the corner of Pleasant and Middle streets. Her shop was for years the gathering place of all the wits and story tellers in the town. The tavern originally stood at 79 Middle street.

Puritan House. Located at the corner of Main and Washington streets is the old Puritan House, one of the first brick buildings in Gloucester, erected in 1810 by James Tappan. It has been known successively as the Tappan Hotel, Gloucester House, Mason House and Puritan House, but during recent years it has not been used as a hotel. During the middle of the nineteenth century all the important social functions of the town were held at this hotel.

Jonathan Lowe Tavern. This tavern originally stood at the corner of Main and Rogers streets The proprietor, Jonathan Lowe, established the first regular communication by coach with Boston, making two trips a week with a two horse open coach. The first trip was made on April 25th, 1788, the arrival of the coach creating a great sensation.

In addition to the ones briefly described there are ten or more fine old colonial houses on Middle street, and others of more or less interest on Washington, Angle and Main streets, and Western avenue.

First Parish (Unitarian)   Prospect St. Methodist Episcopal
Independent Christian (Universalist   Trinity Congregational

Sunday Services at Churches.

Prospect Street Methodist Episcopal church, Rev. Thomas Hancock, Ph. D. pastor. Service at 10.30 a. m.; Sunday school at 12 o'clock, Eben Elwell, superintendent; Baraca Class at same hour; Epworth League devotional service at 6.30 p. m.; evening service 7.30.

Independent Christian church, Universalist, Middle St., Rev. John Clarence Lee, pastor. Morning service at 10.30 o'clock; church school at noon, Robert N. Brewster, superintendent; Young People's Christian Union at 6.30 p. m.

First Parish church (Unitarian), Middle St., Rev. Bertram D. Boivin, minister. Morning service at 10.30 o'clock; Sunday school at close of service.

Trinity Congregational church, corner Middle and School Sts., Rev. Albert A. Madsen, Ph. D., minister. Service at 10.30 a. m.; Sunday school at noon; men's class, 12.10 p. m.; intermediate Christian Endeavor at 5.15; Christian Endeavor at 6.15; evening service at 7.30 o'clock.

The Salvation Army, Adjutant and Mrs. Edward W. Shira, officers in command, hall 23 Pleasant street. Sunday school 11 a. m.; Young People's Legion at 6.45 p. m.; gospel service at 8 p. m. preceded by outdoor meeting at 7.30 o'clock.

First Baptist
Our Lady of Good Voyage, Portuguese Catholic

St. Ann's Roman Catholic
St. John's, Episcopal

Sunday Services at Churches.

St. Ann's Catholic church, Pleasant street, Rev. William J. Dwyer, permanent rector. First mass at 6.15 a. m., second mass at 8.30; children's mass at the same hour; high mass at 10.30 o'clock.

Church of Our Lady of Good Voyage, Portuguese Catholic, Prospect street, Rev. Francis Vieira DeBem, pastor. Morning mass at 8.30 a. m., mass at 10.30 o'clock.

St. John's Episcopal church, Middle street, Rev. J. H. C. Cooper, rector. Holy Communion at 8 o'clock; service with sermon at 10.45; evening prayer at 7.30 o'clock.

First Baptist church, Pleasant and Middle streets, Rev. Arthur W. Warren, pastor. Service at 10.30 a. m.; Bible school at noon, Frank Rowe, superintendant; Young Men's Bible Class at same hour, Sumner Vibert, leader; Christian Endeavor at 6.15 p. m.; evening service at 7.30 o'clock.

First Church of Christ, Scientist, Grand Army hall, Washington street. Services at 10.30 a. m.; Sunday school at 11.45 a. m. Reading room open daily, except Sunday, at 16 Pleasant street, from 2.30 to 4.30 p. m.

Unloading Fish

Copyright,
Frank L.

The Fisheries.

The name of Gloucester has been associated for centuries with the Fisheries, it was the pioneer in that industry in America and still stands foremost in the pursuit of that and associated industries. Almost from the time when the first settlement was established in 1623, fishing has been the principal occupation of the people and it is estimated that as many as ten thousand persons were employed in this industry and its various branches when the business reached its highest point a few years ago.

Fishing voyages along the coast in the early days were dangerous undertakings, for besides the menace of storms and rough weather the fishermen were often attacked by the Indians and the French. The active pursuit of fishing as an industry may be said to date from about 1710 when voyages began to Cape Sable and beyond to the Grand Banks about 1741, at which time seventy vessels were engaged in the fisheries.

At the beginning of the Revolution the industry was in a thriving condition, about six hundred men being employed in it. The war, however, destroyed the business and the fisheries declined steadily, reaching their lowest ebb from 1820 to 1840 In the meantime commerce had greatly expanded. The cod take had supported, in the eighteenth century, an extensive trade with Bilbao, Lisbon, and the West Indies, and though changed in nature with the decline of the Bank fisheries after the war, it continued to thrive through the first quarter of the nineteenth century

About 1850 the fisheries began to revive and under the influence of better prices for the catches, improved methods, and the discovery of

THE GLOUCESTER BOOK

Mending Nets

new fishing grounds, it has continued to grow until today Gloucester's fishing fleet numbers several hundred vessels that cover the fishing grounds from the Capes of Virginia to Greenland and Iceland.

From some points across the harbor in East Gloucester the skyline of the city has a strangely foreign look and the impression becomes

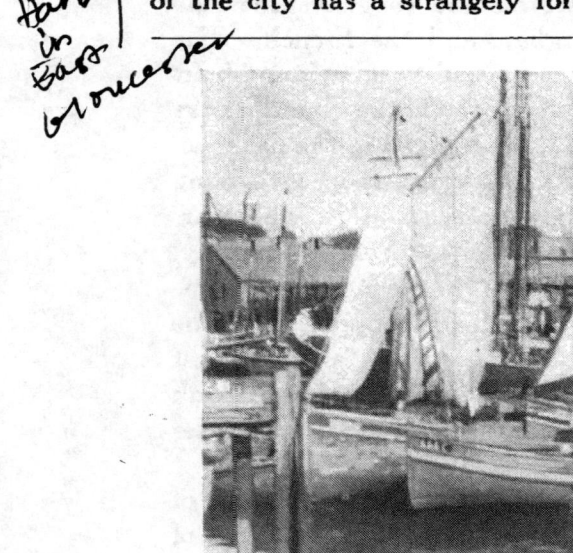

Harbor is East Gloucester

THE FISHERIES 49

almost a reality when one meets large numbers of Italian and Portuguese along the waterfront. The Italian and Portuguese sections of the city form a considerable percentage of the population, the most of whom are engaged in the fisheries.

The life of a fisherman has always been a hazardous occupation but, fortunately, through the greater efficiency of the skippers and crews and

Talking It Over

the improvements in the type and sailing qualities of the vessels which are engaged in the industry today, the loss of life in late years has been greatly reduced.

One of the greatest dangers the fisherman has to contend with on the fishing banks is the heavy fogs which sometimes settle down very suddenly and the fishermen in their dories become separated from their vessel and lost sometimes for days, perhaps exhausting their supply of food and drink in the meantime, until they are at length picked up by a passing vessel or succumb to exposure.

One of the worst years for the fishing fleet was in 1879, when twenty nine vessels and two hundred and forty-nine lives were lost. During 1920 with over two hundred vessels engaged, five vessels and eleven men were lost.

In the words of Chaplain Russell of the Fishermen's Institute "Only

THE GLOUCESTER BOOK

hardy souls can gather the food of the seas for the children of men. They must toil in fair weather and in foul, and often brave an angry sea. These fishermen of the great deep are more then fisherfolk. They belong to the great army of peace, and serve where the danger is greatest because human need is also great. Let us ever hold them in grateful remembrance, these men who labor and give their lives in their task of administering for their fellow-men the bounties of God."

Once a year, in midsummer, a memorial service is held for those who have lost their lives at sea and flowers are strewn on the waters at Blynman bridge that the outgoing tide may bear them to their silent graves in the great deep.

Kent + Bellows + Images of Monhegan Matinicus.

Story of the Esperanto

In the autumn of 1920 a challenge was sent to Gloucester by the Halifax Herald, offering a cash prize of $5,000 and a trophy to the winner of a race between the fastest Gloucester fishing vessel and the Canadian "Delewana." The race was to be known as the first "International Fishermen's Race" and was to be sailed under the following conditions: The entrants must be full fledged fishing schooners, carrying ordinary sail, usual weight duck, and manned by a crew of not more than twenty-five men, the captain of whom must have had at least one year's experience in fishing on the banks. The vessels could carry only their ballast of iron or stone, and no racing equipment could be added. The usual vessels must not exceed 150 feet in length. The race must be sailed before Nov. 1st, 1920.

Mr. Benjamin Smith of the Gorton-Pew Fisheries accepted the challenge and picked the "Esperanto" to defend the traditions of old Gloucester in the coming race, and Captain "Marty" Welch was chosen to sail her.

As the time for the race approached the interest increased and it became a feature story in the news of this country and Canada. In the meantime the "Esperanto" was being thoroughly overhauled and a crew was being picked to sail her.

On October 25th, the "Esperanto" with as fine a crew as ever sailed out of Gloucester, amid the shouts of thousands of people that lined the waterfront and the shrieks of whistles, was slowly towed out into the channel and down the harbor, and with all sails set, swept by the breakwater on her way to Halifax and to victory.

The rest of the story is too well known to be repeated here it is enough to say that she won both races and the series by a thrilling display of seamanship and plain nerve, over a forty mile triangular course.

On their return Captain "Marty" and his crew were the guests of honor at a banquet, attended by many of the prominent citizens and Governor Coolidge.

The International Fishermen's Race is to be an annual affair but whatever boat and whoever the crew may be that will win the races

STORY OF THE ESPERANTO

The Esperanto

in the future, the first and greatest glory will always be to the "Esperanto" and the gallant crew that sailed her to victory.

Every lover of the sea and of Gloucester regrets the untimely fate of the gallant vessel but all are glad to know that none of the crew were lost when she was wrecked off Sable Island on May 30th, 1921.

Summary Colonies.

Summer Colonies.

By reason of its natural rugged beauty, its admirable location, the picturesqueness of its water front, and the magnificent summer climate, Gloucester has long since taken its place as the ideal summer resort of New England. To point out any particular charm which Gloucester may hold for the summer visitor would be extremely difficult for its attractions are many and of sufficient variety to satisfy the most exacting critic.

It is annually visited during the summer months by upwards of twenty thousand people from all corners of the globe and over one thousand families have their summer homes within the boundaries of Cape Ann.

Annisquam is one of the prettiest summer resorts on the North Shore with a beautiful outlook over the valley of the Squam river and Ipswich Bay. The village reminds one somewhat of the little towns in the Lake District of England. The name Annisquam, is of Indian origin and a number of relics have been dug up during excavations for houses which would seem to prove that the Indians once had a settlement here. While very little is known of the early settlers it is known that fishing was at one time carried on quite extensively from this little town and several of the old stone wharves are still in existence. The Annisquam river, running from Ipswich Bay to Gloucester harbor with branches running to Riverdale and West Gloucester, has delightful little summer colonies at Wheeler's Point, Thurston's Point, Riverview, Wolf Hill, Winniahdin, Stanwood Point, and Fernwood, while a number of small islands in the river furnish ideal locations for summer camps. The Annisquam Willows, forming an arch over Washington street near Vine street, were planted about seventy-five years ago by men by the name of Chard who drove the early stage coach between Lanesville and Gloucester.

SUMMER COLONIES 55

Hawthorne Lane

Mother Ann

Gate Lodge

56 THE GLOUCESTER BOOK

Views of Annisquam and the Marshes
Ipswich Bay

Magnolia was formerly called Kettle Cove. Today it is a section devoted to palatial summer homes and hotels, with a beautiful ocean outlook and picturesque, rugged shores. There are a number of points of interest within walking distance of the town, namely Rafe's Chasm, Norman's Woe, United States Coast Guard Station, Naval Compass Station, and Ravenswood Park, which are described under the heading, "Points of Interest."

Bass Rocks is noted for its rugged boulders and magnificent surf display, especially after a storm. It has a beautiful shore drive and a well laid out golf course. Nearby is Good Harbor beach, affording at all times excellent bathing, and off shore is Thacher's Island with its twin lights, the scene of a tragic shipwreck in 1635 in which twenty lives were lost.

East Gloucester has an artist colony in the summer months running well into the hundreds, some of whom are internationally famous. With their canvases and traps they saunter forth to the picturesque wharves and quaint by-streets, the beaches and rocks, themselves adding much to the general picturesqueness of Gloucester in the summer time. Many art exhibitions are given during the summer, some of the paintings bringing big sums. There are a number of fine hotels in this section, from the large, fashionable ones to the small "homey" one of more modest rates.

There are many other sections such as Eastern Point with its magnificent summer homes, interesting walks and drives, Brier Neck, which has been developed into a thriving colony in the past few years, and Long Beach with its hundreds of cottages and excellent beach of firm white sand.

The Shore at Magnolia

Copyright, 1921
Frank L. Cox

GALLERY ON THE MOORS
East Gloucester

Its doors were opened to the public in September, 1916, for the first Art Exhibition.

For years scores of artists have painted about Gloucester, but their work, housed over a wide area, has been difficult of access to the public. As a means of overcoming this difficulty and to bring the work of the artist before the people, this Gallery was offered as a place of Exhibition. Its aim and ideal is development of truth and beauty in Art, community spirit and freedom from personal influence and ambitions. Its activities have increased incredibly and numbered among the various branches are, an Annual Exhibition of Paintings and Sculpture, Group Shows, Community Theatre, known as the Playhouse on the Moors, including plays, pagaents and classic dancing, a Community Dramatic School, which supplements the theatre as a foundation for future work, Music, Lectures, and Literature in the nucleus of a small library pertaining to Gloucester authors and subjects.

The Gallery extends a welcome to all-- stranger, guest and citizen. The Annual Art Exhibitions are held in August, free to everyone. Groups of plays are held in July and the latter part of August.

Front Beach, Rockport

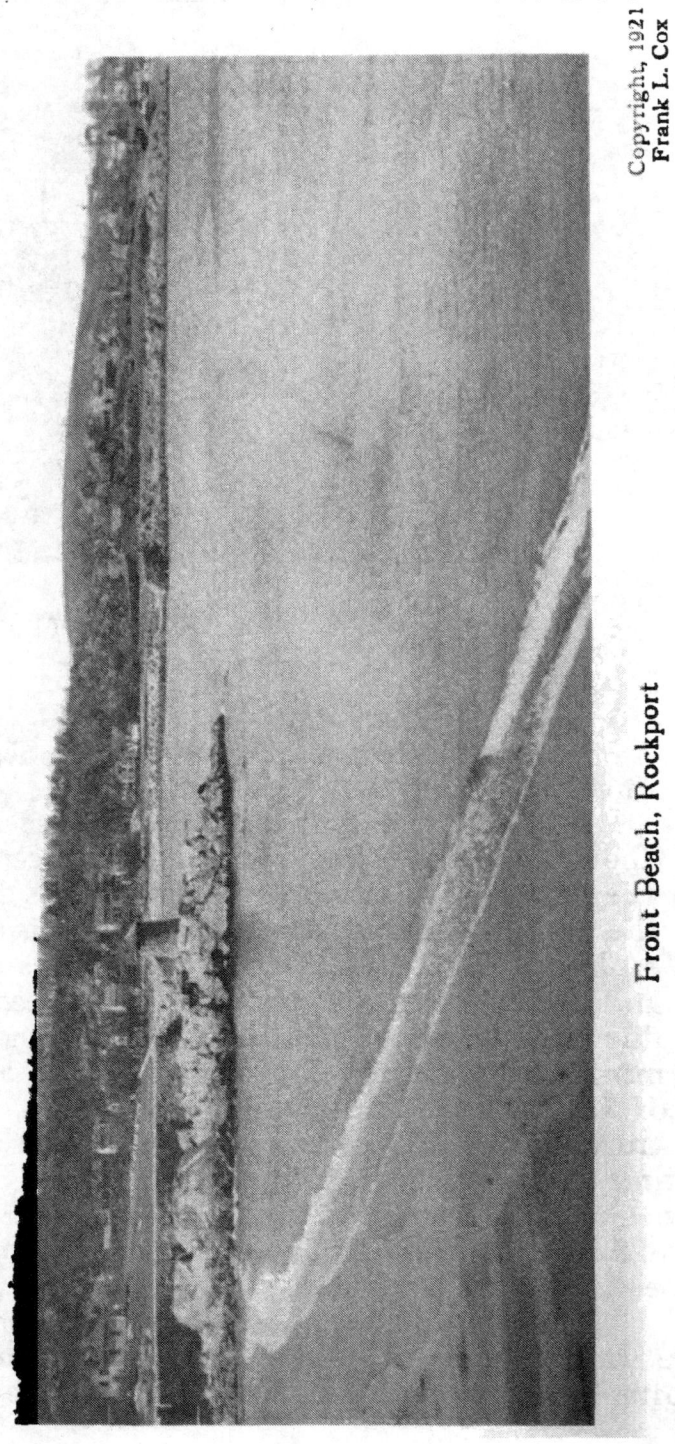

Copyright, 1921
Frank L. Cox

Rockport.

Rockport, or Sandy Bay, as the town was formerly called, was a part of Gloucester until 1840 when it was incorporated and set up its own town government. Like Gloucester, its inhabitants early engaged in the fishing industry and as early as 1743 we read that "Ebenezer Pool, John Pool and Benjamin Tarr, with such others as should join with them, had liberty to build a wharf at the Whirlpool, so called; and also so much of the Neck called Bearskin Neck as is sufficient to set a warehouse on." Not possessing the facilities for large vessels the pursuit of this industry has been largely confined to the shore fisheries, the trapping of lobsters forming the major portion of the business as carried on today.

Rockport granite is known the country over and the quarries at Rockport, Pigeon Cove and Bay View produce many thousands of tons of this valuable stone each year furnishing employment to several hundred workmen. The industry dates from about 1823, when the quarries were first worked, and has furnished granite for government fortifications and navy yards, Boston custom house tower, Woolworth building in New York, and Brooklyn bridge.

The summer colony has grown considerably in the last twenty years, for a cleaner and more wholesome town in which to spend the summer cannot be found in New England. There are a number of good beaches, a beautiful shore drive, and the ocean scenery is unsurpassed. Many artists make their home here during the summer months and find interesting subjects to transfer to their canvases along the quaint old wharves and rugged shore.

The breakwater erected by the government has given Rockport a safe harbor, available for large vessels of all types, and the town is often visited during the summer by some one of the fleets of U. S. warships.

Gloucester Fishermen's Institute

The Social Center of the Fishermen of the North Atlantic.

ENTRANCE, FISHERMEN'S INSTITUTE.

Many of the men employed in the fishing fleet are away from home while in Gloucester. The Fishermen's Institute is the center for these men while ashore and provides the following for their recreation and convenience:—lodging rooms, lunch counter, baths, pool tables and reading room

The fishermen receive their mail at the Institute and all writing material is furnished free of charge.

A series of twenty-one Sunday evening entertainments is given each year.

A non-sectarian institution for all men of the sea.

GLOUCESTER FISHERMEN'S INSTITUTE.
8 Duncan St., Gloucester, Mass.

ITALIAN FISHERMEN

Young Men's Christian Association

The Gloucester Y.M.C.A. is a center for men's and boys' work among the industries, schools, churches, U. S. Navy and other groups throughout Cape Ann. It has a well organized Automobile School, Gymnasium Classes, Swimming Pool, Recreational and Game Rooms, Tennis Club, Dormitories, general information bureau and special boys' rooms with organized social, educational and religious work; has a special department of service for assisting summer residents and visitors, with Secretary to assist in organizing beach sports and game activities. There is also a department assisting in employment matters and information regarding hotels, etc.

Open twenty-four hours a day while U. S. Naval Vessels are in port and from 9 A.M. to 10 P.M. the rest of the season.

A cordial welcome is extended to all visitors to Gloucester.

Gloucester points with pride to the Gloucester National Bank, Gloucester's most historical banking institution.

It is a pleasure to refer to the history and success of this old banking institution, which was chartered in 1796, during the second administration of George Washington as president of the United States. It has withstood every financial and business panic since that time.

It is the oldest bank in the city, the second oldest bank in the state of Massachusetts, and the eighth oldest bank in the United States.

Its present home, on Post Office Square, is the finest architectural structure in our city. It is equipped with the most modern and up-to-date vault of manganese steel, the only known metal to resist the most modern cracks man.

It is one of the show places of our city, and visitors are extended a most cordial invitation to inspect the building and bank equipment.

The Gloucester Safe Deposit & Trust Company was chartered by the Commonwealth in 1891 and commenced business in February, 1892.

Through progressive and modern banking methods, the Trust Company soon took the lead in banking circles of Gloucester and, today, ranks as the largest financial institution of this city. It maintains facilities for all branches of banking and also has a large Trust Department.

Visitors to Gloucester are urged to make this institution their banking home during their stay.

Index to Advertisements.

FISH AND FISH PRODUCTS
    Parkhurst Fisheries Co.
    Frank E. Davis Fish Co.
    Gold Bond Packing Co
    Interstate Fish Corporation

INSURANCE
    F. J. Babson & Co.
    Cunningham & Kerr
    Richard C. Steele
    Johnson

COAL
    Gloucester Coal Co.

GARAGES
    Hart Garage Co., 15 E. Main street
    Perkins & Corliss, Inc., Western avenue
    Roy Reed, 67 E. Main street

STATIONERS, BOOK DEALERS, NOVELTIES, ETC.
    The Waiting Station, 114 Main street
    Jeffery's Stationery Store, 12 Pleasant st.

CLOTHING
    R. Cameron, Jr., (Men's and Boys') 15 1-2 Elm street
    Perry's Haberdashery, (Men's) Main street
    The Greater New York Store, (Ladies) 211 Main street

DRUGGISTS
    Junction Pharmacy, Inc., 388 Main street
    Gorman Drug Co., 195 E. Main street

PLUMBING, HARDWARE, ETC.
    L. E. Smith Co., 221-223 Main street
    L. D. Lothrop, (Marine Hardware) 70 Duncan street

INDEX TO ADVERTISEMENTS

ART GOODS, PICTURE FRAMES
    Mother Ann Picture Parlor, 50 1 2 Main st
    Nunes' Art Store, 8 Centre street

MUSIC, ETC.
    Fred W. Peabody, 195 Main street

MILLINERY
    Alice Bentley, 101 Main street
    Wonson & Holt, 65A Middle street
    Mrs. Ricker, 18 Pleasant street

SPORTING GOODS, AUTO SUPPLIES
    Charles J. Gray, Main street
    W. F. Whitmarsh, Inc.
    Rockport Auto Supply Co.

TAXI SERVICE
    Sawyer's, Telephone 120

HOTELS AND DINING ROOMS
    Hotel Savoy
    Wonasquam Lodge, Annisquam
    Gorman's Restaurant and Dining Room
    The Tavern

LUMBER DEALERS, CONTRACTORS, ETC.
    D. C. Ballou, Contractor, Tel 272-M
    Gloucester Lumber & Trading Co.,
        32 Maplewood avenue

CIGAR MANUFACTURER
    M. Rose, 12 Hancock street

SHOES
    Manufacturers Shoe Outlet, 173 Main st.

PATRONIZE
    Ye Judith Sargent Tea Room, 49 Middle st.

REAL ESTATE
    Jonathan May, Magnolia, Mass.

FRUIT
    James F. Patten's Sons, 82 Main street

WILLARD BATTERY SERVICE
    Gloucester Storage Battery Station, 19 E.
        Main street.

SEND FOR DESCRIPTIVE PRICE LIST
—MAIL ORDER DEPARTMENT—

GOLD BOND PACKING CO.
PURVEYORS OF
HIGH GRADE FISH SPECIALTIES

Mackerel, Herring, Codfish, Tongues and Sounds, Salmon, Sea Moss
Canned Fish: Oysters, Shrimp, Clams, Sardines, Crab Meat, Soft Shell Crabs

GLOUCESTER, MASSACHUSETTS.

Sawyer's Taxi Service
'PHONE 120

Seven Passenger Cars To Let by Hour, Day or Trip
Taxi Service at All Hours

Stand: Savoy Hotel

MILLINERY

Alice Bentley

101 Main St.

Gloucester, - - Mass.

Tel. 1429-M

(Successor to A. B. Murray)

WONASQUAM LODGE
"THE HOUSE OF COMFORT"

Fine Ocean View   Clean, Sandy Beach
Safe Bathing, Boating and Fishing
Excellent Table   Private Baths

——*June to October*——

FRANK H. SHUTE, Prop.   .   .   .   ANNISQUAM, MASS.

Ladies' and
Children's Garments

Dresses a Specialty

Men's and
Boys' Clothing

R. Cameron, Jr.

15 1-2 Elm Street

Opp. Tel. Block   Tel. Con.

Live and Boiled Lobsters

FRESH FISH

Produced Daily From Our Traps

Deliveries Made Anywhere

Interstate
Fish Corporation

Rockport, Mass.

Office Supplies   Dennison's Supplies

Jeffery's Stationery Store

12 Pleasant St., Gloucester

Quality Developing and Printing
Eastman Kodaks

GRANITE SAVINGS BANK
ROCKPORT, MASS.
Incorporated 1884

Last Interest Rate FIVE per cent. Interest begins first business day of every month. Your account will be appreciated.

W. F. WHITMARSH, INC.

BICYCLES, CAMERAS
SPORTING GOODS

AUTOMOBILE TIRES AND ACCESSORIES

48-50 AND 53 MAIN STREET

TELEPHONE 976-M　　　　　　　　　　GLOUCESTER, MASS.

For a real Mild Smoke

TRY THE

8c ALPINE 8c
xx　　　　xx

The Cigar of Quality, strictly long filler imported Sumatra wrapper.

M. ROSE, Mfr.,

12 HANCOCK ST.　　　GLOUCESTER.

L. E. Smith Company

Plumbing

Heating

Hardware

Kitchen-ware

Vessel Supplies

221 and 223 Main Street
Gloucester, Mass.

MOTHER ANN PICTURE PARLOR

Colored Photographs, Oil Paintings, Finished Pictures,
Hand Carved Frames, Pictures Framed, Renewed, Etc.

══════ J. W. THOMAS ══════

Telephone 1179-R.　　　Open Saturday Evening

50 1-2 Main Street　　　　　　　Nearly Opposite Strand The
　Up One Flight　　　　　　　Look for the Sign of Mother An

We make Serving Trays, all sizes, to order and carry Handles.

Salt Mackerel, Codfish, Fresh Lobster
—— SOLD DIRECT TO FAMILIES THROUGH MAIL ORDERS. ——

A Most Attractive and Interesting Place To Visit

Frank E. Davis Fish Co.'s Headquarters Rogers St., Gloucester, Mass.

THE "latch string" is always out---visitors are always welcome here. Come in and see how the tasty mackerel are prepared---watch the interesting process of preparing codfish---see how we serve over 100,000 families all over the country with the choicest ocean food.

Motor or drive on good roads, right to our door---we are ready to show you everything.

We have a special assortment of sea foods selected for summer use, that is very popular. This makes a delightful souvenir to send to friends, especially inland folks. If it is inconvenient to call, allow us to mail you our latest "Descriptive Fish List."

Your copy of our new book, "Seafoods---How to Prepare and Serve Them" is free.

FRANK E. DAVIS FISH CO.,   Central Wharf, Gloucester, Mass.

Tel. 1789-W

Gloucester Storage Battery Station

All Makes of Batteries Repaired and Charged

WILLARD SERVICE

East Main St., Gloucester, Mass.

Rockport Auto Supply Co.

✖ ✖ ✖

AUTOMOBILES

AND EVERYTHING TO DO WITH THEM

✖ ✖ ✖

AUBURN TIRES and TUBES

Nunes' Art Store

8 CENTRE ST.,

GLOUCESTER, - - MASS.

A full line of Winsor and Newton, Rembrandt, Cambridge and other makes of colors always on hand at reasonable prices.

OIL PAINTINGS AND MIRRORS RESTORED

Artists' Materials and Hand Carved Frames a Specialty

PICTURE FRAMING

The Tavern

Gloucester, Mass.

A MODERN INN CATERING TO TOURISTS

Insure with Johnson

The Greater New York Store

211 Main Street, - Gloucester.

Coats, Suits, Skirts, Waists, Dresses, Bathing Suits, Sweaters, Furs.

A. SOLOMON, Prop.   Tel. 469-M

Manufacturers Shoe Outlet

173 Main Street
Gloucester, Mass.

GOOD SHOES

at the right price for
Men, Women and Children

Perry's Haberdashery

The Leading Men's Store

Where Style Reigns

Gray's Sporting Goods House

KODAKS
FILMS AND SUPPLIES
DEVELOPING
PRINTING
ENLARGING
SPORTING GOODS
OF ALL KINDS

Lobsters   Steaks   Fish Dinners

Gorman's Restaurant

142 Main Street

Gloucester's
Newest and Best Dining Room
On Second Floor

Quality   Service   Home Cooking

L. D. LOTHROP & SON,

70 DUNCAN ST.
GLOUCESTER

THE PLACE TO GO FOR

Motor Boat Supplies, Oars, Marine Hardware, Fishing Tackle, Cordage, Fishermen's Outfits of all kinds.

MILLINERY

DRESS HATS
TAILORED and SPORT HATS

Everything that's new in the Millinery Line

PRICES REASONABLE

WONSON & HOLT

65A MIDDLE ST.

Next door to Pattillo's Furniture Store.

THE HAT-CRAFT SHOP

SPECIALIZING IN

Originally Designed Parlor Products

and

SPORT GOODS of the FINER KINDS

Mrs. Ricker
18 Pleasant Street

DR. ARTHUR SMITH,

Osteopath

MASONIC BLDG.,

201 Main St.,   Gloucester, Mass.

Telephone 862-R

In the course of Business throughout the years you will nee many new arrangements of Printing and your ideas can be con veniently and economically conveyed thru our service of

Designing   **Printing**

Engraving   **Binding**

Consult

White & Gaffney, Inc.,

Printers of "The Gloucester Book"

Telephone 1675-M

75 Maplewood Avenue   Gloucester, Massachu

ADVERTISEMENTS

TELEPHONE   GOODS DELIVERED

James F. Patten's Sons

Wholesale and Retail
Dealers in

Foreign and Domestic

FRUIT

82 Main Street,

GLOUCESTER, - - MASS.

Perkins & Corliss, Inc.
Tel. 200
Gloucester

Ford Authorized
Sales and Service
Gasoline, Oil and
Full Line Tires and
Accessories

Perkins & Corliss, Inc.
Tel. 200

The HOTEL SAVOY

European Plan

GLOUCESTER, - MASS.

Open the year round.

STEAK, CHICKEN AND SEA FOOD
DINNERS

BROILED LIVE LOBSTER
OUR SPECIALTY

Cunningham & Kerr

All Kinds of

Good Insurance

Cunningham & Kerr

The Agency of Service

MAGNOLIA

Seashore Estates
Cottages
Bungalows
Shops

JONATHAN MAY,

Shore Road,   Magnolia, Mass.

Tel. 426-R

Have your

PRESCRIPTIONS

filled at the

GORMAN DRUG CO.

195 East Main St.,
East Gloucester,   -   Mass.
Tel. 683-M

We consider the filling of prescriptions and handling of medicines a most serious and important thing.

Dealers in All Kinds of

JUNK

Highest Prices Paid
For All Kinds of Junk
Prompt Attention
Given to All Orders
Twenty-four Service

GLOUCESTER LUMBER & TRADING CO.,

Philip Michaelson, Pres.

TEL. 21.

---

32 MAPLEWOOD AVE.

Gloucester Lumber & Trading Company

Dealers in all kinds of New and Second-Hand Building Material.

Wreckers of Buildings: Nothing too Large or Small.

TELEPHONE 21.

RICHARD C. STEELE

INSURANCE

Junction Pharmacy, Inc.
388-390 Main St.,
Gloucester, - - Mass.

*When Looking for
Home Made Candies
We Suggest*

COZY
CORNER
CANDIES

STATIONER

Complete Line of
SCHOOL AND OFFICE SUPPLIES
SOUVENIRS AND NOVELTIES

BOOKSELLER AND NEWSDEALER
——WHOLESALE AND RETAIL——

Agent for Boston and New York Daily and Sunday Papers.

The Waiting Station,

F. M. SHURTLEFF,

4 Main Street, - - Gloucester, Mass.

YE JUDITH SARGENT
TEA ROOMS AND GIFT SHOP
IN THE HISTORIC SARGENT-MURRAY-GILMAN HOUSE

At ye shop and tea room ye can tell it not only with flowers but with novelties, prizes, gifts, pastries, cakes, candies and all good things to eat.   Luncheons served.

OPEN DAILY FROM 11 TO 6 EXCEPT SUNDAYS

49 MIDDLE STREET,
GLOUCESTER,   -   MASSACHUSETTS.

D. C. BALLOU — CONTRACTOR
Concrete and Stone Construction Work

Sand, Gravel and Loam Delivered Anywhere

—MAKER OF CEMENT BLOCKS—

Office and Pit: Eastern Ave.
Telephone 272-M

Residence: Magnolia, Mass.
Telephone 480

FRED W. PEABODY

195 Main Street, Gloucester, Mass.

Pianos ❧ Talking Machines ❧ Kodaks and Camera Supplies

ROY REED

Local Agent for
CLYDESDALE and ATLAS TRUCKS

AUTOMOBILE AND MOTOR BOAT REPAIRING

GASOLINE and CYLINDER OILS

CARS FOR HIRE
STORAGE AND SUPPLIES

GARAGE

67 East Main Street   Telephone 1348   Gloucester, Mass.

F. M. SHURTLEFF
Bookseller and Newsdealer
114 Main Street
Gloucester,   Mass.
SOLE DISTRIBUTORS OF
The Gloucester Book

CPSIA information can be obtained
at www.ICGtesting.com
Printed in the USA
BVHW011332210621
610132BV00010B/294